D1368505

IRISH
in America

IRISH

in America

James E. Johnson
with Jack Kavanagh

Lerner Publications Company • Minneapolis

Page 2: Irish-American tailors in Cincinnati

1994 REVISED EDITION

Library of Congress Cataloging-in-Publication data

Johnson, James E., 1927–
    Irish in America / James E. Johnson: with Jack Kavanagh. —
1994
        p. cm. — (In America series)
    Includes index.
    Summary: Discusses the experiences of Irish immigrants
to the United States, their assimilation into American
society, and their culture.
    ISBN 0-8225-1954-2 (lib. bdg.)
    ISBN 0-8225-3475-4 (pbk.)
    1. Irish Americans — Juvenile literature. [1. Irish Americans.]
I. Kavanagh, Jack. II. Title. III. Series.
    E184.I6J6 1994
    973'.049162—dc20   93-25991
                                                  CIP
                                                   AC

Manufactured in the United States of America

7 8 9 10 – I/MP – 01 00 99 98 97 96 95 94

CONTENTS

INTRODUCTION

On St. Patrick's Day, Irish Americans—everyone from children to leprechaun look-alikes—proudly display their heritage.

One wonders that there are any Irish in America at all. No nation's emigrants have longed for their homeland as ardently as the Irish. As John McNulty observed about his fellow Irish Americans in *The New Yorker* magazine, "Generations after their ancestors left Ireland, their descendants yearn to return to a place where they have never been."

England, France, and Spain sent colonists to the New World (North, South, and Central America) to conquer it. The conquerers were driven by ambition. European kings and queens measured their success by how much land their armies claimed for the crown. But Ireland had no kings. Its ancient royal rulers had fallen while defending the island from British invaders. The Irish people were forced from their land by foreign rulers and famine. They traveled to North America—both Canada and the United States—not to expand the British Empire but to escape English injustice.

The flow of Irish immigrants to the United States began early in the 19th century. The flow became a flood in 1845, when blight destroyed Ireland's potato crop, the staple food of the Irish people. The blight caused a terrible famine—tens of thousands died of starvation. Landowners—mostly British—were indifferent to the suffering of their tenants. With no hope for relief at home, the desperate Irish peasants literally fled for their lives—many seeking refuge in America.

The Irish came ashore in North America's port cities—most landing in New York and Boston—and clustered there in squalor. The tyranny of the landlords from whom the Irish had fled was nearly matched by the hostility of many Anglo Americans (Americans of English heritage). The newcomers were ridiculed and attacked for their nationality as well as their Catholic faith. Help-wanted signs frequently included the warning, "No Irish Need Apply."

Throughout the 19th and well into the 20th century, immigration from Ireland to the United States was large and constant. Bound together by their Catholicism, the Irish united through churches, schools, and social clubs. They gradually worked their way into the fabric of American society. A flair for political organization gave Irish Americans power beyond the number of their votes.

The children and grandchildren of the early Irish immigrants blended into America's "melting pot." By the mid-20th century, the Irish American had become hard to distinguish from the German, French, or

An Irish-owned grocery store in Philadelphia, late 19th century

Swedish American. Intermarriage hastened the "extinction" of the Irish American.

Despite the forces of the melting pot, a new Irish-American pride is visible and growing. Americans have a renewed interest in Irish music, step dancing, Gaelic (the traditional language of Ireland), and Irish customs and history. Irish culture is celebrated in American restaurants, bars, and specialty shops. On March 17, Americans of all ethnic backgrounds celebrate St. Patrick's Day with parades and Irish music. Some people even drink green beer and wear buttons that say "Kiss Me, I'm Irish."

By some estimates, at least 60 percent of all Americans have some Irish ancestry. A few Irish

The McGovern family, from County Cavan, Ireland, found a new home and a new flag in the United States.

Americans—even those with an obvious Irish family name—are unaware of their heritage. Others are indifferent. But most Irish Americans are proud of their ancestry—at least on St. Patrick's Day.

American tourists flock to Ireland—many to trace their family's roots and others to visit relatives. Ireland is no longer "far across the sea," as the homesick Irish immigrants once sang. Today visitors can reach the island by a short transatlantic flight. Aer Lingus, the Irish airline, will gladly carry you "back where you have never been."

Milwaukee's Irish Fest features big-name Irish and American entertainers and draws more than 100,000 visitors every summer.

1
FAREWELL TO ERIN

Irish peasants lived in cramped cottages with thatched roofs.

Thousands of Irish people crossed the sea to come to America during the 18th century. Many of these immigrants were Protestants, originally from Scotland. They had occupied farmland in the northern counties of Ireland, seized by the British in war. Primarily farmers or craftspeople, these "Scotch-Irish" went to North America seeking economic opportunities. They found success in their new land, proving to be talented government officials and industrial leaders.

Unlike the Scotch-Irish, most of Ireland's people practiced the Catholic religion. Oppressive laws, passed by the British government during the 18th century, made

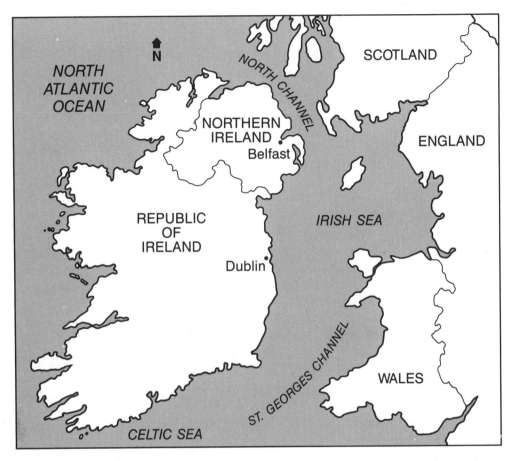

it difficult for Catholics to succeed in Irish society. Few Catholic families owned their own land. Most were cotters—peasant farmers who worked a landowner's property. Rents were high and country people often feared they would be evicted from their homes.

Rural life was hard for all. Peasant cottages were built of wood, stone, and sod, usually with a dirt floor. People slept on straw mats and sometimes shared quarters with their most precious possessions—the livestock. They ate meagerly from a diet of potatoes, milk, and herring. They grew vegetables in a garden near the house. A pig—fattened on potato peelings for later slaughter—and a few hens or ducks—kept to provide eggs or a rare holiday meal—rounded out the food supply.

Present-day Ireland is split into two nations: Northern Ireland and the Republic of Ireland. Irish people sometimes call their nation Erin. Because the countryside is so green, Ireland is also known as "the Emerald Isle."

Life in the cities was not much better. Dublin, the largest city in Ireland—with a population of 175,000 in 1830—was filled with slums. Many streets were unpaved and lacked any sort of sewage system. Wages were low, rents were high, and working people had little hope for advancement.

In the early 19th century, Irish Catholics began to set out for America—several thousand each year. They hoped to find wealth, land, and a better life in the United

St. Kevin's Church in Glendalough. In Ireland, as in the Irish-American neighborhoods, the Catholic church was the center of community life.

States, but they also regretted leaving Ireland. The experience of many poor immigrants is described in a verse from this Irish folk song:

> The landlords and their agents
> Their dogs and their bailiffs
> The land of our forefathers
> We were forced to give o'er
> Now we're sailing on the ocean
> For honor and promotion
> And parting with our sweethearts
> It's them we do adore

The Great Famine

The giant flood of people from Ireland to North America began in 1845, when the potato, the crop on which the Irish people depended, failed to grow. People began to starve. Nearly three-quarters of a million people died of starvation or disease during the five-year crisis.

A few private organizations in England, such as the Quakers and other religious groups, tried to provide food to the starving people. Relief organizations set up public kettles of gruel but were able to feed few of the hungry. As the potato famine worsened, many Irish peasants became desperate. The number of able-bodied people capable of caring for the dead and dying dwindled. Some died of starvation. Others fell to diseases such as typhus, dysentery, and cholera. More than a million fled Ireland.

Although hunger drove the Irish from their homes, they also fled a tyrannical government. The British viewed the Catholic faith of the Irish people with disdain. During the 18th century, Catholics were forbidden by law to own land, vote, teach school, and sell books. Gradually, many of the oppressive laws against Catholics were lifted. But at the time of the famine, more than half of the farmland in Ireland was still owned and controlled by British landlords.

When the Irish began to starve, their anguish was ignored by the landowners. Landlords not only allowed

Shipping lines advertised cheap passage from Ireland to New York.

tenants to go hungry, they added to the peasants' plight by evicting thousands of families from their homes during the crisis.

Many Irish people saw only one way to relieve their suffering. They could go to America. The British government, eager to be rid of the starving people, encouraged them to leave—arranging for ships that would transport passengers across the Atlantic Ocean at low fares. Some landlords even paid their tenants' passage. In desperation, the peasants abandoned their own country and sought hope in a new one.

The United States, an ocean voyage away, looked like a land of opportunity. The young country needed laborers. Boston, New York, and Philadelphia were growing centers of commerce. Streets had to be built and sewers dug. Railroads were spanning the land.

A 19th-century family in Ireland

Canal diggers in Lawrence, Massachusetts

Canals would link the rivers and lakes of inland America with eastern seaports. There was work to be done, and the Irish were eager to do it. If the immigrants could survive the ocean crossing and find a foothold in the port cities of America, they could begin a new life. In the United States, the immigrants believed, hard work would be rewarded.

People were also encouraged to leave Ireland by their friends and relatives who had already left. The earliest immigrants sent letters home, often telling of high wages, cheap farmland, and freedom from military service in America. In Ireland 30 acres of land was considered a large farm. In the United States, 100-acre farms were common. Some immigrants wrote of daily meals that a family in Ireland would see only on holidays. One folk song, inspired by such glowing reports of America, said:

> They say there's land and work for all
> And the sun shines always there

Those Irish people who had achieved a degree of success in America often sent money to their relatives back in Ireland to pay for the ocean voyage. But the settled Irish Americans often failed to warn the next wave of immigrants of the perils ahead.

An emigrant ship leaves Belfast for America in 1852.

In the spring and early summer of 1847, the roads to the Irish coast bustled with activity. People pressed toward seaport towns where they could buy a ticket for a ship. Few Irish people really wanted to leave their country. Most felt they had no choice. To stay in

16

Ireland meant death. This sad farewell was written by one Irish poet:

> Farewell to thee, Erin mavourneen
> [Ireland my darling]
> Thy valleys I'll tread never more
> This heart that now bleeds for thy sorrows
> Will waste on a far distant shore
> The green sods lie cold on my parents
> A cross marks the place of their rest
> The wind that moans sadly above them
> Will waft their poor child to the West

Across the Wide Atlantic

A voyage across the Atlantic Ocean in a mid-19th-century sailing ship was a treacherous experience. If winds were unfavorable, the trip to America could take as long as 10 weeks. Even the fastest voyages took more than a month. Shipowners kept fares low by cramming as many passengers as possible into tight quarters below deck. Often the immigrants were denied any comfort at all. Food supplies were meager and sometimes rotten. Toilet areas were odorous. Drinking water was also scarce—and too precious to use for bathing or washing clothes. Diseases like typhus and yellow fever swept through the ships. Burial services for those who died on the way to America were routine, and transports soon earned the nickname "coffin ships."

But when the ships neared land, the passengers became filled with excitement. They expected paradise, and the harbors of North America gave a promising first impression. The Irish looked with awe at the shorelines of New York, Philadelphia, and Boston. When they went ashore, some travelers emptied small packets of Irish soil onto the ground. The gesture symbolized the wedding of Ireland and America.

Railroads took Irish settlers west. Here, travelers celebrate as the first locomotive crosses the Alleghany Mountains.

2
LIFE IN A NEW LAND

Once in the United States, the Irish soon discovered they had not entered paradise. Americans were quick to take advantage of the newcomers. In fact, the Irish were even exploited by their own kind. Irish-American "runners," con artists who spoke with familiar Irish accents, led the new arrivals to overpriced lodging houses. Pretending to be helpful, the runners betrayed their countrypeople, often stealing their money or selling them phony train tickets. The immigrants were forced to take any available job to buy themselves out of debt.

Castle Garden was the point of entry for early Irish immigrants to New York.

In 1851 more than 200,000 Irish people reached the shores of America. With as many as 40 immigrant ships arriving in a single day, government officials in New York and Boston tried to cope with the influx. Doctors boarded incoming ships and gave brief medical examinations. Nearly 20 percent of the passengers carried an infectious disease. Many of these passengers were immediately sent to special hospitals where they were quarantined, or isolated, so disease wouldn't spread among the general population.

In 1855 New York City established a building called Castle Garden as a point of entry for immigrants. There, the Irish were temporarily safe from runners and other cheats. Immigrants could buy food, rail tickets, and lodging at a fair price. Immigration officials gave advice and assisted children who were traveling alone to join relatives in America.

The Birth of Irishtown

Most Irish immigrants settled in the city. They often had no choice. They were usually penniless when they reached America's port cities, so they squeezed into any dwelling they could find and took any job available. Irishmen and boys took laboring jobs. They dug ditches, paved roads, and hauled freight. Young Irish women became household servants and nannies. Both men and women took low-paying jobs in mills and factories.

Living conditions were harsh in the large cities as well as in the smaller industrial towns rising around America's urban centers. Factory workers crowded into row houses, built one against another. Entire families lived in one-room apartments. Many dwellings lacked light, fresh air, and running water.

The most serious danger in the immigrant neighborhoods was the lack of sanitary facilities. Outhouses often overflowed and sewage seeped into the streets. Garbage was put outside to decay and rot. Drinking water was often polluted. Disease ravaged the poor.

Smallpox broke out among the Irish-American community in 1845. In 1849 a cholera epidemic spread along the East Coast of the United States. More than 500 of the 700 people who died were Irish.

Many Irish Americans became discouraged and regretted the decision to leave their homeland. At times they felt that everything and everyone was working against them. If they had survived the perilous ocean crossing, they had to face the runner who wanted to swindle them out of what little money they had. The crowded slums and factories of New York and Boston seemed to offer far more dangers than they did opportunities.

Despite these discouragements, the immigrants stayed in America and worked to improve their lives. They set up self-help associations like the Hibernian (Irish) Society for the Relief of Emigrants and the Irish Emigrant Society of New York. These groups exposed dishonest boardinghouse keepers and gave advice and financial assistance to travelers.

Many Irish women became nannies and housekeepers.

Irish clam diggers in Boston

While they still longed for the beauty of "the Emerald Isle" and the quiet life they had left behind, the Irish gradually adjusted to their new home. Soon they transformed America's tenement neighborhoods into thriving "Irishtowns"—rich with the language and customs of Ireland.

Irish laborers lay railroad track near Cleveland, Ohio.

The Irish Go West

Most but not all Irish immigrants settled in the large cities of the eastern seaboard. Some set out for the inland territories of North America. They traveled by train to Chicago, Detroit, and St. Louis. A few took overland trails as far west as California, where the goldfields promised quick wealth. Others farmed the land. Accustomed to village life, many Irish-American farmers hated the open spaces and loneliness of the midwestern prairie. One Irishman yearned for the tight-knit community he had left behind:

> I could then go to a fair, a wake, or a dance...I could spend the winter's nights in a neighbor's house cracking jokes by the turf fire. If I had there but a sore head I could have a neighbor within every hundred yards of me that would run to see me. But here everyone can get so much land...that they call themselves neighbors that live two or three miles off.

Many Irish immigrants made their home in the midwestern territories.

For single Irishmen, inland construction projects offered many job opportunities. The United States was growing. Settlers were building cities across the continent and connecting them with roads and railroads. Laborers were in high demand, and Irish immigrants became part of America's expanding workforce.

Construction companies recruited Irish workers by advertising in the Catholic newspapers of eastern cities. Employers also recruited workers directly from Ireland—enticing them with promises of high wages. A job in the United States paid as much as $1.50 a day. In Ireland a person lucky enough to find a job would accept that amount for a week's work.

The life of a construction worker wasn't easy. Dishonest employers used numerous schemes to avoid paying workers a fair wage. If rain kept the men from working, no one was paid. But they were still charged for daily food and lodging in the overpriced rooming houses provided by the construction company. Canal diggers often stood knee-deep in chilly water. Diseases such as dysentery, cholera, and malaria were common

Railroads recruited workers directly from Ireland.

Laborers drill for oil on the American prairie.

at construction sites. Laying railroad track was dangerous work that included blasting tunnels through rock and rugged terrain. Accidents and cave-ins caused many deaths. A popular 19th-century saying claimed that an Irishman was buried under every American railroad tie.

The Anglo-American Backlash

Even after the famine in Ireland subsided, Irish immigrants continued to flock to America—as many as 50,000 per year. By 1860 half the foreign-born population of New York City was Irish. Soon there were more Irish people in New York than in Dublin. Neighborhoods like South Boston in Massachusetts and New York's Greenwich Village were inhabited largely by the Irish working poor.

Early Irish-American communities, like this neighborhood in New York City, were rough shantytowns—often plagued by overcrowding, poverty, and disease.

As Irish Americans grew in numbers, they soon aroused the fear and prejudice of Anglo Americans. As early as the 1830s, the Irish had encountered violence and hostility in America. They were despised more for their religion than their nationality. In 1840 there were 663,000 Catholics in the United States. A decade later, with the influx of immigrants from Ireland, Catholics numbered 1,606,000 (about 7 percent of the American population).

Anglo Americans cast cruel stereotypes on the Irish. Many Irish people lived in poor neighborhoods that were plagued by crime, illiteracy, and alcoholism. Some Anglo Americans claimed that these by-products of poverty were typical traits of *all* Irish people. Other Anglo Americans feared that Irishmen and women would take their jobs, since, desperate for employment, Irish immigrants would work for low wages. And the Irish were organizing politically. Among other goals, the Irish in America wanted their native country to be free from English rule. They hoped for a war between

Irish immigrants in a midwestern town (above). A coin commemorates the 1836 founding of the Ancient Order of Hibernians in America (left).

the United States and Britain that would bring freedom to Ireland. This continued insistence on war with England angered many Anglo Americans.

Anglo Americans feared that Irish laborers, like these weavers in a New England factory, would drive down wages.

Such controversy actually shaped a political party in the 1850s. The Know-Nothing party, officially called the American party, objected to immigration and opposed the election or appointment of Catholics to government posts. Meetings were held secretly, and the party earned its nickname when members replied "I don't know" to questions about the group's activities. The Know-Nothing party nominated a candidate for president in 1856. He made a poor showing in the election, and the party quickly faded into the background of the American political scene. Discrimination against Irish Catholics, however, did not fade from American society.

27

3
A CALL TO ARMS

Throughout the early 19th century, northern abolitionists had been working to end slavery in the United States. In 1861, rather than free the African-American slaves who worked their farms and plantations, 11 southern states broke from the United States and formed the Confederate States of America. President Abraham Lincoln called the northern states to arms to save the Union.

Irish immigrants had a mixed response to the Civil War. Most Irish people had settled in the North. They had brought their hatred and loathing of British rule to America with them. And England, which imported cotton from the southern states, supported the Confederacy.

Although British support of the South should have inflamed the Irish Americans, they did not automatically support the northern cause. The hatred of England was tempered by a fear that freed African-American slaves might take jobs from Irish workers. In addition, many Irish Americans saw little difference between the suffering of slaves in the South and hardships endured by factory workers in the North. The Irish in America were preoccupied with their own problems. They endured so much misery in the slums of New York City and Boston that they felt indifferent to the plight of black Americans.

Yet when President Lincoln called for volunteers to join the Union army, many Irishmen responded. Governor John A. Andrew of Massachusetts wrote the United States secretary of war in 1861: "Will you authorize the enlistment here…of Irish, Germans, and

President Lincoln found that many Irishmen wanted to fight for the Union.

Irish-American Mathew Brady (far right) headed a team of photographers who gave us dramatic images of the Civil War.

other tough men? We have men of such description, eager to be used, sufficient to make three regiments."

The number of Irish in the Union army has been estimated at between 150,000 and 170,000 men. Irish soldiers fought fiercely—though perhaps for the promise of a good fight rather than a commitment to ending slavery. Northern generals George Meade, Philip Kearny, and Philip Sheridan were among many Irishmen who rose to prominence during the Civil War.

The Irish Brigade

The most acclaimed of the Irish units in the Union army was the Irish Brigade, part of the Army of the Potomac. The brigade was made up of the 23rd, 29th, 69th, and 88th New York regiments, together with the 116th Pennsylvania and the 28th Massachusetts. Each regiment carried a green flag, often decorated with Irish slogans and Irish symbols like the harp and the shamrock. Captain Thomas Meagher was put in command of the brigade and was promoted to brigadier general.

General Philip Sheridan

The Irish Brigade took part in many famous Civil War battles, fighting bravely at Gettysburg, Fredericksburg, and Chancellorsville. At Antietam, Maryland, 1,200 Irishmen marched in tight formation into an entrenched Confederate line. The charge forced a retreat by the southern forces, but the action was costly. Only 500 Irishmen survived and only 280 of them were able to appear for inspection the next day. A soldier of the 118th Pennsylvania Volunteers, to whose rescue the Irish Brigade had come, wrote of the valor of the Irish Americans:

Most Irishmen joined the Union army of the North. But some— those who had settled in the South—joined the Confederacy.

> The gallant Irishmen moved into battle array with the precision of parade. Prominent in its place beside the national standard, the green harp of Erin was distinctly observed....The dead and wounded strewed the ground, thickening as the distance from the enemy lessened. Twice and again the green standard fell, but only to be promptly seized again.

Enough of Your Hard Fighting

The bravery and loyalty of the Irish Brigade aside, Irish Americans reacted with widespread anger to President Lincoln's Emancipation Proclamation, which freed the slaves in 1863. Tension between Irish Americans and African Americans had been growing throughout the war. In April 1863, black men were employed to break a bitter strike led by Irish-American dock workers. Then, with the Union suffering heavy losses, the federal government passed a draft law to induct additional men into the army. This action inflamed Irish Americans even more. The law allowed a man to buy his way out of military service by paying a replacement to serve for him. Most Irishmen were laborers who could not afford the $300 required to hire a substitute.

The first draft lottery, held on July 11, 1863, produced a list of 1,200 names—the majority of which were Irishmen. Following the publication of the list, Irish workers in New York City gathered at draft centers and vacant lots. When the New York police department attempted to disperse the crowds, the workers attacked. Police Superintendent John Kennedy, himself an Irishman, was badly beaten. The rioting continued for four days. Irish-American mobs roamed the city, attacking the armory on Lexington Avenue and the homes of merchants and civic leaders. Hundreds were killed.

The main targets of the rioting Irish were African Americans. New York's Colored Orphan Asylum was burned, many blacks were beaten, and others were hanged. In their frustration, the rioters had simply turned their anger upon people who were less fortunate than themselves.

The Irish had come to the United States for a better life. But instead of peace and prosperity, the newcomers found war and prejudice. The conflict left some immigrants feeling bitter and betrayed. The experiences of many Irishmen are relayed in this traditional folk song:

Paddy's Lamentation

It's by the hush my boys
I'm sure that's to hold your noise
Listen to poor Paddy's lamentation
I was by hunger pressed
And most bitterly distressed
So I took a thought I'd leave the Irish nation

So I sold my horse and plow
I sold my sheeps, my pigs, and sow
My little farm of land and I departed
And my sweetheart Biddie McGee
I'm feared I'll never see
For I left her back at home quite broken hearted

Then me and a hundred more
To America sailed o'er
Our fortunes to be making we were thinking
But when we landed in Yankee land
They stuck a rifle in my hand
Saying Paddy, you must go and fight for Lincoln

General Meagher to us said
If you get shot or lose a leg
Every mother's son of you will get a pension
But in the war I lost my leg
And all I got was a wooden peg
Oh boys, this is the truth to you I mention

Here's, to you boys, do take my advice
To America I'd have you not be coming
For there's nothing here but war
Where the murdering cannons roar
And I wish I was back home in dear old Erin

General Thomas Meagher, commander of the Irish Brigade

Irish immigrants to America found a country torn apart by war.

The Irish worried that freed African Americans would compete with them for laboring jobs.

The Tammany Society, which came to be dominated by Irish politicians, holds a ball in New York City.

The O'Brien family of Stevens Township, Minnesota, 1915

4
IRISH *AND* AMERICAN

Construction projects soared after the Civil War.

With the war between the states over, Irish Americans went back to work—in factories, mines, and mills, on farms and on the railroads. Irish laborers played an important role in the construction of the transcontinental railroad, the Brooklyn Bridge, the Statue of Liberty, and other American landmarks built during the late 19th century.

Settlers continued to move west across North America—the Irish among them. Irish Americans like Jesse James, Butch Cassidy, and William "Buffalo Bill" Cody would become some of the most famous and colorful figures of the Old West. All across the nation, Irish people began to move into the mainstream of American life.

Buffalo Bill Cody thrilled Americans with his Wild West shows.

The Massachusetts state militia confronts striking Irish-American mill hands, members of the International Workers of the World.

The Irish Take a Stand

Although they were beginning to assimilate into the larger American culture, Irish people retained strong links to their heritage. They founded Irish-American hospitals, insurance funds, schools, labor associations, and churches. They joined societies such as the Ancient Order of Hibernians in America and the Friendly Sons of St. Patrick. Newspapers, the *Irish World* and the *Irish Echo,* addressed issues of importance to Irish-American people.

While most Irish groups worked peacefully, a few used violent tactics to achieve their political and social goals. One militant group that made headlines after the Civil War was the Irish Republican Brotherhood, also known as the Fenians. Active in both Ireland and the United States, the Fenians hoped to incite an uprising of the Irish people and to free Ireland from British rule.

In Ireland the Fenians struck out against British authorities with bombings and other terrorist acts. Meanwhile, the American Fenians attempted to invade Canada, then a British territory. On June 1, 1866, under the command of John O'Neill, an 800-man Fenian army captured Fort Erie, Canada, near Niagara Falls. The Canadians reacted with a hastily assembled militia of 2,000 men but were beaten back. The Fenians were veterans of the Civil War and experienced soldiers. O'Neill then led his small army back to Buffalo, New York, only to be captured by military forces of the United States. Two later raids on Canada were also unsuccessful. Several Fenian leaders were tried and imprisoned, but the cause of Irish independence was not forgotten.

Another bloody battle took place during the 1860s and 1870s in the coal mines of Pennsylvania. Unjust treatment and dangerous working conditions led Irish-American miners to form an organization known as the Molly Maguires. Named after a legendary Irish heroine who fought British landlords during the 1600s, the Molly Maguires wanted higher wages, better working conditions, and the right to join and organize labor unions.

The Molly Maguires were secretive and violent. They struck out at mine owners with threats, beatings, and killings. Fatal "accidents" were arranged to punish miners who betrayed the organization. Many miners felt caught between the Molly Maguires and the mine owners. Workers dared not speak out against the coal bosses, for fear of losing their jobs. They dared not oppose the Molly Maguires, either, lest they be labeled traitors.

Mine owners, determined to prevent the workers from organizing, hired Allan Pinkerton, a private strike breaker, to wipe out the Molly Maguires. Pinkerton employed a young Irishman, James McParlan, who passed himself off as a miner and infiltrated the secret organization. His records were used as evidence when 19 members of the Molly Maguires were tried and hanged for crimes against the coal bosses.

Children labored for low wages under dangerous conditions in coal mines, prompting groups like the Molly Maguires to strike out against the coal bosses.

Radicals and Reformers

The Molly Maguires were destroyed, but Irish-American laborers continued their fight for fair treatment. Along with Americans of many ethnic backgrounds, they joined the Knights of Labor, the American Federation of Labor, and the Industrial Workers of the World. Irish Americans like Mary Harris "Mother" Jones and Elizabeth Gurley Flynn (known as "the Union Maid") led the fight for workers' rights.

Mother Jones (left) championed workers' rights, while Margaret Sanger (above) led the birth control movement.

In rural regions, Irish Americans joined the National Grange, which worked on behalf of the American farmer. The Grange was founded in 1867 by an Irishman named Oliver Kelley. The Populist party, another grassroots political group of the late 19th century, was led by the Irish-American writer Ignatius Donnelly.

Margaret (Higgins) Sanger, the daughter of an Irish immigrant, was a leader in the struggle for women's rights. In the early 20th century, she fought to make birth control readily available to all American women.

Irish workers demanded fair pay and better working conditions.

41

In the West, Irish laborers like these Arizona miners sometimes felt threatened by competition from Mexican and Asian workers.

Nellie Bly (born Elizabeth Cochrane in 1867) was a crusading journalist who sometimes went "undercover" to get a story. As a reporter for the *New York World*, she brought public attention to the plight of America's factory workers, mental patients, prisoners, and tenement dwellers. Her articles helped fuel the social reform movement at the turn of the century.

While some Irish Americans championed the rights of the poor, others displayed bigotry toward them. The Irish sometimes resented newer immigrants to the United States—those from Eastern Europe and Asia. Like the Irish before them, the newcomers were viewed as unfair competition who would work for low wages. They were often ridiculed for their unfamiliar accents, religious practices, or foreign way of dress.

The Mahoney family lived comfortably in a midwestern city (left), while the crowded tenements of the eastern seaboard became home to newer European immigrants (below).

During the 1880s, an Irishman named Dennis Kearney led a hostile movement against Chinese laborers on the West Coast. He promoted such slogans as "the Chinese must go" and "America for the Americans." Kearney's leadership was ironic considering the prejudice his own people had faced earlier in the century. But the Irish were no longer outsiders in the United States. While their loyalty to Ireland remained strong, they were beginning to view themselves as Americans.

City Hall and Beyond

Throughout the 19th century, Irish immigrants continued to arrive in America. They were no longer driven by famine, however. They came, as did immigrants from other countries, looking for a better life. When the new immigrants arrived, they found thriving Irish-American communities. By the late 1880s, Boston was about 50 percent Irish American and Chicago about 25 percent. Irish Americans didn't live in the slums of the central city any longer, though. New arrivals—Jews,

William Kiley sells turkeys at this market in Lawrence, Massachusetts.

Irish-American police officers, posing here in 1925, show off their turn-of-the-century uniforms in New York.

Italians, Poles, and Slavs—were pouring into America's inner cities. Meanwhile, the Irish were moving into the American middle class—yet their communities retained a strong ethnic flavor.

Irish Americans filled every job category imaginable. They became shopkeepers, schoolteachers, trolley-car drivers, and carpenters. They worked in stockyards, foundries, and factories. The Irish were prominent in civil service (government) jobs, particularly on city police and fire-fighting forces.

But certain professions, such as law and medicine, were sometimes shut off to Irish people. Anti-Catholic prejudice had not disappeared in the United States. The Ku Klux Klan preached hatred of Catholics and other minority groups. Quota systems limited the number of Catholics admitted to private colleges and professional schools. (Italian, German, and other Catholics also suffered from this discrimination.)

The Magees of Philadelphia, late 19th century

Mayor Richard Daley ran Chicago's city hall for more than 20 years.

Al Smith served as governor of New York before his unsuccessful bid for the presidency.

In 1928 Alfred E. Smith, the first Irish Catholic candidate for president, was defeated at the polls. Smith's Catholicism was a factor in his defeat. (As late as 1960, some voters refused to support President John F. Kennedy because he was Catholic.) Well into the 20th century, a distinctly Irish surname such as O'Brien, Flynn, or Fitzpatrick could still pose a stumbling block to advancement in American society.

Despite such prejudice, Irish people generally found success in politics. They joined the Democratic party in great numbers. A gift for political organization enabled the Irish to dominate city councils and capture city halls. In 1873 "Honest John" Kelly took over the infamous Tammany Hall administration of New York City. He became the first in a long line of powerful Irish-American "bosses."

Throughout the 20th century, Irish mayors ran America's big cities: Jimmy Walker in New York City,

James Curley in Boston, Richard J. Daley in Chicago, Thomas Pendergast in Kansas City, and Frank Hague in Jersey City. Irish Americans also influenced state and national politics, running successfully for governorships and Congress. James A. Farley, chairman of the Democratic National Committee, managed the political career of President Franklin D. Roosevelt in the 1930s. When John F. Kennedy became president in 1960, he and his closest advisers were jokingly called "the Irish Mafia."

President John F. Kennedy and his wife, Jackie (left). Robert Kennedy (below).

Success through Education

The same issue that often stirred up hatred toward the Irish—their Catholicism—was an important factor in their success in the United States. As soon as enough Irish families had moved into a community, they built a church. Churches offered more than just religious services, though. The Catholic church was the center of Irish-American life. Priests were community leaders, and marriage outside the Catholic faith was strongly discouraged.

Many Irish-American families sent their children to public schools. But many more Irish children attended private parochial schools, where they learned about the Catholic religion as well as academic subjects. Irish Americans did not object to prayer in the classroom. They insisted on it!

Father Michael McGivney (above) founded the Knights of Columbus, an association of Roman Catholics, in 1882. St. Patrick's Cathedral (above, left) was opened in New York City in 1879.

As the Irish in America grew in numbers, they established seminaries to train young men for the priesthood. With private colleges often closed off to them, Irish Americans also founded Catholic universities. Although established by French priests, the University of Notre Dame in Indiana has educated thousands of Irish Americans. In fact, the school's athletic teams carry the nickname "the Fighting Irish."

By establishing schools of medicine, law, architecture, and engineering, Irish Americans were able to enter fields that had once been off-limits to them. By the middle decades of the 20th century, barriers to individual achievement had finally been cleared away for the Irish. Lawyers and doctors with Irish surnames were commonplace. Irish Americans became leaders of business and industry. Some, like automobile pioneer Henry Ford, were among the most powerful people in the world.

Schoolteacher Kathryn Murphy

Henry Ford and his son Edsel pose with the first (left) and the 15 millionth Ford automobile ever made.

The Shamrock Club Color Guard parades at Milwaukee's Irish Fest (left). An Irish dancer laces up her shoes (below).

Forever True

By the 20th century, many Irish Americans had never seen Ireland. They were the descendants of Irish immigrants. They considered themselves wholly American. But despite their assimilation into American society, Irish Americans did not forget their homeland. Ireland's struggle for independence continued, and American groups like the Friends of Irish Freedom and Northern Aid backed the cause with donations and political involvement.

In 1920 the British Parliament split Ireland into two nations, north and south, and granted each nation some powers of self-government. Northern Ireland, a largely Protestant region, accepted the division and the terms of self-rule. Citizens in the Catholic South, though, wanted nothing less than full independence. They continued their struggle for freedom from England. Although partial independence was granted in 1922, not until 1949 did the southern counties of Ireland finally sever all ties with Great Britain and become the Republic of Ireland.

Hatred of the British government has not disappeared in Ireland. Many Catholics in Northern Ireland feel oppressed by the Protestant majority and continue to strike out against British authorities. Terrorism and violence are common occurrences in the streets of Northern Ireland.

Most Irish Americans hope for a peaceful solution to the problems in Northern Ireland. Many work with Project Children, a group that allows young people from war-torn Northern Ireland—both Catholic and Protestant—to spend their summer vacation with an American family. In operation since 1975, Project Children has given thousands of children a chance to escape the fighting in Northern Ireland and has fostered greater communication among Irish people of all religions—and on both sides of the ocean.

Irish Americans demonstrate against oppression in Northern Ireland.

The Drovers, made up of Irish and Irish-American musicians, keep Irish traditions alive.

The New Irish

Frustrated by limited job opportunities in their own nation, thousands of Irish immigrants still come to America each year. Not all of these newcomers enter with permission of U.S. immigration authorities, though. Unable to get "green cards"—permits to reside legally in the United States—many Irishmen and women live and work in the United States secretly.

In 1990 Congress amended the U.S. Immigration and Nationality Act, increasing the number of green cards set aside for Irish people. With this amendment, many "illegal Irish" will be able to become legal residents, and many more native Irish people will be able to immigrate legally. Indeed, more than 150 years after the first immigrants reached America, the United States remains "the land of opportunity" for the Irish.

5
CONTRIBUTIONS TO AMERICAN LIFE

Politicians

Irish Americans have made contributions in every area of public life. In politics one name stands out above all others: Kennedy. Joseph P. Kennedy of Boston was the grandson of a penniless immigrant. He amassed a great fortune as an investment banker and used it to advance the political careers of his sons.

The Kennedy family has known triumph and tragedy. John F. Kennedy was elected president of the United States in 1960 and was assassinated in 1963. Robert Kennedy, attorney general during his brother's administration, was assassinated while campaigning for the U.S. presidency in 1968. The youngest Kennedy son, Edward (Ted), was elected to the United States Senate in 1962. He remains a dominant force in Congress.

In addition to John Kennedy, presidents Ronald Reagan and Richard Nixon are descended from Irish immigrants. President Bill Clinton's Irish roots come from his mother, Virginia Cassidy Kelley. When Clinton became president, he appointed Jean Kennedy Smith, sister of John, Robert, and Ted Kennedy, as ambassador to Ireland. Clinton also appointed Raymond Flynn, Boston's mayor, as ambassador to the Vatican, the center of the Catholic church.

Throughout the last half of the 20th century, the U.S. House of Representatives has been led by Irish Americans such as John McCormack, Thomas P. "Tip"

Ted Kennedy

President Bill Clinton has Irish roots.

53

O'Neill, and Thomas Foley. The U.S. Senate is led by George Mitchell and features among its members Daniel P. Moynihan, John F. Kerry, Robert Kerrey, and Connie Mack III. Irish Americans who have served on the Supreme Court include William J. Brennan and Anthony M. Kennedy.

Although the Irish no longer dominate urban centers, Irish Americans still lead many major cities. Raymond Flynn served as the mayor of Boston from 1984 to 1993, and Richard M. Daley continues a family tradition of leadership in Chicago.

Writers

Some of the most famous names in American literature have been Irish, including F. Scott Fitzgerald *(The Great Gatsby),* Flannery O'Connor *(A Good Man Is Hard to*

F. Scott Fitzgerald (left) and Flannery O'Connor (above) are among America's best-loved writers.

54

Mary Higgins Clark (above) and Tom Clancy (right) are best-selling authors.

Find), and playwright Eugene O'Neill *(Long Day's Journey into Night).* Many of these writers' works draw on their Irish-American heritage. The Irish-American experience is further described in James T. Farrell's *Studs Lonigan* trilogy (1932–1935), Betty Smith's *A Tree Grows in Brooklyn* (1943), and Edwin O'Connor's *The Last Hurrah* (1956).

Many contemporary authors are also Irish Americans. This list includes Tom Clancy, writer of high-tech action novels, Pulitzer Prize winner William Kennedy, crime writer George V. Higgins, mystery writer Mary Higgins Clark, and newspaper columnist Jimmy Breslin.

Artists

Irish Americans have also excelled in the visual arts. Mathew Brady, the son of Irish immigrants, was one of the world's first photographers. He is best known for images taken on the battlefields of the Civil War. Louis Sullivan was a leading architect of the early 20th century. He built some of the nation's first skyscrapers. Georgia O'Keeffe, who died in 1986, was one of America's greatest painters. Her works feature images of the American landscape—including animal bones, rocks, flowers, and desert scenes. Popular cartoonists Walt Kelly ("Pogo") and Chester Gould ("Dick Tracy") were also Irish Americans.

Mathew Brady

Georgia O'Keeffe

Musicians

Many of America's most popular singers and band-leaders have been Irish. Early in the 20th century, George M. Cohan wrote patriotic songs like "Yankee Doodle Boy" and "You're a Grand Old Flag." Kate Smith is best known for singing "God Bless America" during World War II. Bing Crosby set the style for popular singers during the 1920s and 1930s, and Tommy and Jimmy Dorsey were among the best jazz musicians of the big-band era. Eddie Cochran was a rock and roll pioneer.

Ireland continues to export great music to the United States. Contemporary audiences enjoy Irish musicians U2, Van Morrison, Sinead O'Connor, and the Pogues. Americans have also taken a renewed interest in traditional Irish music performed by groups like De Dannan and Clannad.

The legendary Bing Crosby

De Dannan brings the best Irish folk music to America.

Irish import Sinead O'Connor

57

Actors

The motion-picture industry has produced an array of Irish-American stars. Buster Keaton, a pioneer of the silent-film era, was Irish, as were James Cagney, Spencer Tracy, and Helen Hayes. Other Irish-American screen legends include Grace Kelly and Gene Kelly. Present-day film stars Michael Keaton, Shirley MacLaine, Warren Beatty, Matt Dillon, Drew Barrymore, Tom Cruise, Susan Sarandon, Angelica Huston, and Jack Nicholson all trace their roots to Ireland.

Irish Americans have been delighting television audiences since TV was invented. For many years, Americans watched Ed Sullivan showcase new talent on his popular variety show. Americans laughed along with Jackie Gleason and Art Carney on "The Honeymooners" as well as Ed McMahon on "The Tonight Show." Carroll O'Connor of "All in the Family" and Mary Tyler Moore starred in classic TV comedies.

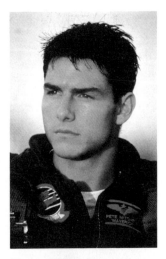

Tom Cruise is a box-office favorite.

Drew Barrymore (left) comes from a famous acting family. Gene Kelly (above) delighted audiences in Singin' in the Rain *and other classic films.*

Nolan Ryan hurls a strike (left). Dream-Teamer Chris Mullin (below)

Athletes

Irish Americans have provided leadership in baseball with such famous managers as John McGraw, Connie Mack, and Joe McCarthy. Nolan Ryan of the Texas Rangers dominated pitching as the 20th century neared its end, and power hitter Mark McGwire of the Oakland Athletics continues a tradition of brawny Irish sluggers.

In basketball the Irish presence is mostly courtside with coach Pat Riley of the New York Knicks and coach Chuck Daly of the New York Nets. Chris Mullin of the Golden State Warriors played for the 1992 Olympic "Dream Team" in Barcelona, Spain. Football's Irish Americans include Buffalo Bill quarterback Jim Kelly, running back John Riggins, and TV sportscaster John Madden, formerly the head coach of the Oakland Raiders.

Irish-American athletes have excelled in individual as well as team sports. Ireland has exported many distance runners to American colleges, the best being Eamonn Coghlan, holder of the indoor mile world

Olympian Nancy Kerrigan

Pat Riley is one of the most successful coaches in the NBA.

John McEnroe has had a stellar tennis career.

record. Nancy Kerrigan was the 1992 Olympic bronze medalist in figure skating, and she won her first national figure skating title in 1993. Jimmy Connors and John McEnroe have ranked among the best tennis players in the world. From the time of John L. Sullivan in the 19th century, many of boxing's heavyweight champions have been Irish Americans.

Name any sport, profession, or creative art, and you are sure to find Irish Americans among its leaders. But the ordinary Irish people have perhaps contributed more to American life than the celebrities.

Irishwomen in Florida, 1904

When the Irish came to the United States, they brought their cultural heritage with them. Irish ballads and fiddle tunes evolved into American bluegrass, folk, and country music. The Irish named their children for the saints of their church. Eventually, Irish first names, such as Sean, Erin, Kevin, and Brian, became popular with non-Irish families too. Irish stew and soda bread moved from Irish kitchen tables to the menus of American restaurants. Wearing green on March 17, whether you're Irish or not, is an American tradition. Most large cities hold a parade on St. Patrick's Day.

American speech has become more colorful with the addition of such Irish phrases as "Top of the morning to you" and "May your shadow never be less." Americans regularly use Irish words like boycott, blarney, and tinker. And in the United States, an Irish blessing applies as widely as it does in Ireland:

Irish dancers wear beautiful costumes.

> May the road rise up to meet you
> May the wind be always at your back
> May the sun shine warm upon your face
> And the rains fall soft upon your fields
> And until we meet again
> May God hold you in the palm of His hand

INDEX

Flynn, Elizabeth Gurley, 40
Flynn, Raymond, 53, 54
Foley, Thomas, 54
food, 11, 15, 61
Ford, Henry, 49
Friendly Sons of St. Patrick, 37
Friends of Irish Freedom, 50

Gaelic. *See* Irish language
Gleason, Jackie, 58
Gould, Chester, 56
Great Britain, 7, 10-11, 13-14, 26-27, 28,
 38, 50-51

Hague, Frank, 47
Hayes, Helen, 58
Hibernian Society for the Relief of
 Emigrants, 21
Higgins, George V., 55
housing: in Ireland, 11; in the United
 States, 20
Huston, Angelica, 58

immigrant ships, 14, 17, 20
Immigration and Nationality Act, 52
Ireland: independence movement of,
 26-27, 38, 50-51; life in, 11-14
Irish Brigade, 29-30
Irish Echo, 37
Irish Emigrant Society of New York, 21
Irish immigration, 7, 10, 12-13, 14-17,
 19-20, 25, 44, 52
Irish language, 8, 61
Irish Republican Brotherhood, 38
Irish World, 37

James, Jesse, 36
jobs, 14-15, 20, 24-25, 35, 45; competition
 for, 26, 28, 42
Jones, Mary Harris (Mother), 40

Kearney, Dennis, 43
Kearney, Philip, 29
Keaton, Buster, 58
Keaton, Michael, 58
Kelley, Oliver, 41
Kelly, Gene, 58
Kelly, Grace, 58

Kelly, "Honest John," 46
Kelly, Jim, 59
Kelly, Walt, 56
Kennedy, Anthony M., 54
Kennedy, Edward, 53
Kennedy, John F., 46, 47, 53
Kennedy, Joseph P., 53
Kennedy, Robert, 53
Kennedy, William, 55
Kerrey, Robert, 54
Kerrigan, Nancy, 60
Kerry, John F., 54
Know-Nothing party, 27
Ku Klux Klan, 45

labor organizations, 38-39, 40
landlords, 7, 11, 13-14
Lincoln, Abraham, 28, 31

McCarthy, Joe, 59
McCormack, John, 53
McEnroe, John, 60
McGraw, John, 59
McGwire, Mark, 59
Mack, Connie, 59
Mack III, Connie, 54
MacLaine, Shirley, 58
McMahon, Ed, 58
McNulty, John, 6
McParlan, James, 39
Madden, John, 59
Meade, George, 29
Meagher, Thomas, 29
military service, 15, 31
Mitchell, George, 54
Molly Maguires, 38-39
Moore, Mary Tyler, 58
Morrison, Van, 57
Moynihan, Daniel P., 54
Mullin, Chris, 59
music, 8, 57, 61

National Grange, 41
neighborhoods, 20-22, 44-45
New York, New York, 7, 14, 17, 20, 25,
 46
Nicholson, Jack, 58
Nixon, Richard, 53
Northern Ireland, 10, 50-51

ACKNOWLEDGMENTS Photographs and illustrations used with permission of the Cincinnati Historical Society, pp. 2, 21 (right); Milwaukee Irish Fest, pp. 6 (left and right), 9, 50 (left, Martin Hintz, and right), 64; Balch Institute, pp. 7, 8, 45 (bottom), 61 (top); Library of Congress, pp. 10, 14, 18, 29 (top and bottom), 30, 33 (top), 39, 40 (left and right), 42, 48 (left); Irish Tourist Board, New York, p. 12; Independent Picture Service, pp. 13, 32, 46 (left), 49 (bottom), 55 (right), 57 (top right); Immigrant City Archives, Lawrence, Mass., pp. 15, 27, 35 (left), 37, 41, 43 (right), 44; Ulster Museum, Belfast, p. 16; National Park Service, Statue of Liberty National Monument, pp. 19, 21 (left), 35 (right); Western Reserve Historical Society, p. 22; Stevens County Historical Society, pp. 23, 24 (bottom), 26 (right), 34 (bottom), 43 (left), 49 (top); Minnesota Historical Society, p. 24 (top); New York Historical Society, p. 25; James Marrinan, p. 26 (left); National Archives, pp. 28, 33 (bottom); Museum of the City of New York, p. 34 (top); Western History Research Center, University of Wyoming, p. 36; The Bettmann Archive, p. 45 (top); Harry Johnson Studio, p. 46 (right); New Bedford *Standard-Times*, p. 47 (left); Office of the Senator, pp. 47 (right), 53 (top); Knights of Columbus, p. 48 (right); Odette Lupis, pp. 51, 61 (bottom); The Drovers, p. 52; Office of the Governor of Arkansas, p. 53 (bottom); Charles Scribner's Sons, p. 54 (left); Farrar, Straus and Giroux / Joe McTyre, p. 54 (right); Simon and Schuster / Bernard Vidal, p. 55 (left); Putnam Publishing Group / John Earle, p. 55 (right); Museum of New Mexico, p. 56 (left); Green Linnet Records, p. 57 (bottom left); Chrysalis / Ensign / ERG, p. 57 (bottom right); Hollywood Book and Poster, p. 58 (all); Houston Astros, p. 59 (left); Golden State Warriors, p. 59 (right); Paul Horvath, p. 60 (top left); New York Knickerbockers, p. 60 (top right); U.S. Tennis Association / Russ Adams, p. 60 (bottom right).

Front cover: Odette Lupis. Back cover: Independent Picture Service.